CZERNOVITZ–CHARMOVITZ

ANETA KAMIŃSKA
Czernovitz – Charmovitz

Translated by
Anna Blasiak
& Bohdan Piasecki

2024

Published by Arc Publications,
Nanholme Mill, Shaw Wood Road
Todmorden OL14 6DA, UK
www.arcpublications.co.uk

Copyright in the poems © Aneta Kamińska, 2024
Translation copyright © Anna Blasiak & Bohdan Piasecki, 2024
Introduction copyright © Anna Blasiak & Bohdan Piasecki, 2024
Copyright in the present edition © Arc Publications 2024

978 1911469 51 3

Design by Tony Ward
Printed in the UK by TJ Books, Padstow, Cornwall

Cover illustration
by Marcus Ward

ACKNOWLEDGEMENTS

The translators wish to thank Tony Ward and Angela Jarman of Arc Publications for bringing Aneta Kamińska's unique voice to an English readership. Their thanks also go to Jean Boase-Beier for her insightful editorial comments on the translations. They are particularly grateful for the trust the poet placed in them, and to her publishers for allowing the reproduction of the poems in Polish.

This book is in copyright. Subject to statutory exception and to provision of relevant collective licensing agreements, no reproduction of any part of this book may take place without the written permission of Arc Publications.

Contents

Introduction / 7

from ZAPISZ ZMIANY (2004)
10 / jeśli nie kawa to • if not coffee then / 11

from CZARY I MARY (2007)
12 / kłuta cięta szarpana • stab cut laceration / 13
14 / gra językowa • language game / 15

from WIĘZY KRWI (2018)
14 / luka • gap / 15
16 / przesadzka • exaggerant / 17
18 / tabunowe tabuwanie • band banding / 19

from CZERNOWITZ CZAROWIDZ (2021)
22 / czernowitz czarowidz • czernovitz charmovitz / 23
24 / [:::] • [:::] / 25

from TERAZ ZARAZ (2022)
26 / koronauczycielka • coronateacher / 27
28 / wzdłuż / wszerz • along / across / 29

from WSCHODNIKI / ZACHODNIKI (2022)
30 / czyja ty jesteś • whose are you / 31
34 / celuję cechuję • i aim i claim / 35
36 / jestem mostem • i am a bridge / 37

from POKÓJ Z WIDOKIEM NA WOJNĘ (2022)
38 / [untitled] • [untitled] / 39
40 / [untitled] • [untitled] / 41
42 / sen mara • all a dream / 43

Biographical Notes / 47

Introduction

Aneta Kamińska has a rather special place in Polish contemporary poetry. She has forged her own poetic style and paradigm. She seems to feel very comfortable in the space between words (and is very good at stretching that space like a balloon and filling it with new / extra meanings) and words seem to gladly submit to her rule. She is a seasoned linguist who plays never-ending language games (based on the sounds, rhyme, rhythm, alliteration and beyond), she juggles meanings, sometimes even contrasting ones, creates new connections or new words (also by contorting or shortening existing ones). It takes an amazing ear and eye to be able to do that – Kamińska sometimes seems like a predator, waiting patiently, observing, but ready to pounce as soon as an opening appears, as soon as the right combination of words comes to the surface, pretty much always hitting the bull's-eye. Some of her linguistic inventions could well take root in the Polish language, they are so precise and so useful, they are so 'right'. And then there is the ambiguity that the poet always plays on, the wonderful multidimensionality.

Kamińska's word games have two principal purposes: they show how far the language can go and display the poet's skill and craft, but they are also the building blocks of a relationship with the reader, providing him / her with moments of sparkling 'a-ha!' when spotting a joke or a ploy. That creates a connection with the poet and with the persona of the poem; it also provides the reader with the satisfaction of having broken a code, of being involved with Kamińska's spectacle of language. The word games fulfil the need to process certain topics in a creative way, but sometimes also the desire to capture historical moments (especially in the last volume, devoted in its entirety to the war in Ukraine). For Aneta Kamińska is a passionate, sharp-penned, courageous chronicler of our times. She doesn't mince words when she is talking about important though difficult things, about tragedies, danger or stupidity. It's all a game for her, which means it'a all a game for us, the readers. But there is also a lot of humour here, a lot of irony.

Kamińska's wordplay stems from a foregrounding of sound in her writing, a way to transfer performative elements of poetry to the page. It is hard not to imagine her poems read out loud. This is important: for Kamińska, sound constitutes more than an aesthetic. It is, instead, a device for the exploration of ideas, a way to give thoughts a structure. Rhyme and rhythm have the appearance of playful free association, a way to add music to poems and find humour in wordplay, but for her they are often an architectural choice, load-bearing, important enough to bend language around them. The importance attached to the music of her language gives rise to Kamińska's characteristic neologisms and justifies her carefree approach to grammar and syntax.

Such poems are particularly exciting for us as translators, because they make it easy to do away with tired romantic metaphors of fidelity and loss in translation. We saw the vastly different versions we produced initially as a celebration of multiplicity, of the many-faceted Polish of Kamińska's verse. The English texts in this collection function as a record of a negotiation between two of many possible readings, rather than the results of a doomed quest for something identical to a perfect original.

And just as well: wordplay and neologisms are keystones of Kamińska's poetics. She uses them to give her writing a propulsive music, as a source of humour and play, and as shortcuts to meaning. Take for example the poem 'Band Banding'. Its Polish title is 'Tabunowe tabuwanie'. The first word means herd-like, and contains the Polish words 'tabu' (taboo) and 'nowe' (new). It evokes an animalistic group engaging in something forbidden, something new: a way to stake out the territory for a text which explores sex, fear, masculinity, femininity, desire, repression... After much deliberation we chose 'band', a homophone of 'banned', but also a term for a group of people and a herd, a flock... It gave us the option to follow up with banding, an unusual term for grouping people together, and a reflection of the echo effect in the original. In the same poem, the Polish line 'z pokalania na pokalanie' is a play on 'pokolenie' (generation) and 'niepokalana' (immaculate), an unmistakable gesture to the unattainable ideal of the virgin birth presented to Catholic women as a model to imitate. We debated 'degeneration' for a while, but the religious overtones seemed too important, hence our choice of 'maculation' in the final version in English.

Another poem, 'Gap', is written in a seemingly child-like language. The biggest difficulty while translating it was finding a solution for Kamińska's term 'kilkunielatki' from the second line, a play on 'kilkulatek', which means a child who is a few years old. But she adds 'nie' there in the middle, a negative. After several attempts, we arrived at 'young-nones', which also contains the negative, however 'young' is less specific than the Polish 'kilkulatek'.

In 'Coronateacher' another difficulty awaited us. The lines 'krzyż krzyczy / i żebrze o masaż' play on a duality of meaning of the Polish word 'żebrze', which can relate to 'żebrać', 'to beg' and / or to 'żebro', a rib. Alas this duality of meaning was lost in translation and we ended up compensating for this loss with more alliteration.

In her books Kamińska creates distinct sets of poems – linked by themes and by sounds. This is one of the reasons why we decided to keep the poems in this collection in chronological order, so that we could retain the delineation of particular sets.

We would like to thank Aneta Kamińska, as well as Tony Ward and Angela Jarman of Arc Publications for letting us go on this translatory adventure. We also want to express gratitude to the Polish publishers of Kamińska's books for allowing us to translate and also reproduce the Polish versions of her poems. These are: Staromiejski Dom Kultury (the publisher of: *zapisz zmiany, czary i mary, więzy krwi*), Fundacja Duży Format (*czernowitz czarowidz, teraz zaraz*) and KIT Stowarzyszenie Żywych Poetów (*wschodniki / zachodniki, pokój z widokiem na wojnę*).

Anna Blasiak and Bohdan Piasecki

jeśli nie kawa to

którą
kupujemy jest mieszanką wielu (najładniejsze) z różnych
(najbardziej jędrne) tylko niektóre składają się
wyłącznie (teraz nożem) najszlachetniejsza odmiana
　　parzona (na pół
i jeszcze) niezwykle
delikatna
w smaku
(sok spływa po palcach) jej aromat intensywny
　　przedziwnie trwały pochodzi
z (klei
się)
dojrzewa na
najwyższych (puszyście i mlecznie)
najlepsze warunki
do

i już
i liż

mnie
(teraz
albo nic)

(orange mocha, cube café)

if not coffee then

> *The language of gourmet coffee meets a confidently sensual, seductive discourse, until it becomes difficult to tell one from the other. We were lucky that Polish and English both use 'now or never' and 'all or nothing', and so our blended idiom at the end was able to follow Kamińska's urgent word game closely.*

which
we buy is a blend of many (prettiest) of various
(firmest) only the finest selection combined
exclusively (use the knife now) the finest varietals brewed
    (in half
and again) uniquely
subtle
taste
(juice runs down fingers) the intense and unusually lasting
    flavour comes
from (it feels
sticky)
ripens at
the highest (soft and milky)
the best conditions
for

so quick
now lick

me
(now
or nothing)

(orange mocha, cube café)

kłuta cięta szarpana

w nastroju wybitnie kobiecym
(drażniąco
czerwonym podrażnionym) odznaczam
się na śniegu
(tutaj zawsze śnieg osiada na szybie zatrzymuje się o włos też
czerwony) przedzieram się przez granice
drzwi furtek ogrodzeń
(windy kursują rzadziej i wolniej niż schody nawet
z szóstego piętra nawet z lękiem i z wysokości) bronię się
walczę
kulę
(plamiąca poplamiona
płynna) wdrapuję siebie
na peron
(lód i chrapiące powietrze gwiżdże i sapie)
prosto
pod pociąg

z dziurą w brzuchu
ranna

pkp warszawa włochy, 28 lutego 2005'gra językowa

stab cut laceration

> *Czary i mary, from which this poem is taken, is a surreal hypertext, containing poems, snippets of dreams, quotations, all of which are shown simultaneously and can be read in any order. The book uses various typefaces and there are also hyperlinks, reminiscent of the largest hypertext – the Internet. One of the book's main themes is illness, present in this poem and also in reproductions of the author's medical tests illustrating the book.*

in a tremendously feminine mood
(jarringly
reddened maddened) i leave marks
on the snow
(here snow always settles on the windowpane and stops a hairline away
also red) i push through borderlines
of doors gates fences
(the lifts are less frequent and slower even than the stairs even
from the sixth floor even with fear and even from height) i defend myself
i fight
i crouch
(staining stained
spilling) i clamber
onto the platform
(ice and raspy air whistles and wheezes)
straight
under the train

wound a hole in my
stomach

warszawa włochy station, 28 February 2005

gra językowa

pulsuję
się sobą i w brzuchu
pod skórą pod
powierzchnią na wierzchu
szukają się ścieżki
dostępu trzaskają i skrzypią łącza mokre są włosy
zlepione kosmyki schylają się
spadają
teraz jeszcze i już

(chcesz się podlizać?)

weź mnie
na wszystkie języki jakie tylko
    masz   znasz
i czytaj

luka

leżakujące podkołdrujące
kilkunielatki

wiesz jak to się nazywa

language game

This poem, like others in this collection, uses a language of computer-like commands. The ambiguity and variety of styles creates a mixture which, according to the poet, reflects our everyday reality, but also remains mysterious. The corporeality, described here in detail, is also an invitation and an opening to pass to a different realm. The matter-of-fact easily turns into the erotic, with a sprinkling of linguistic games.

I pulsate
within myself and in the belly
under the skin under
the surface on the surface
access paths seeking each other
connections crack and creak hair is wet
strands stick together slink
sink
now and again and already

(are you lapping up?)

take me
in all the languages that you
show   know

go ahead and read me

gap

Więzy krwi, from which this poem comes, is a book which becomes a poetic voice of femininity, and also a voice of clear and strong rebellion against patriarchal society and its rules. We follow a girl's journey through childhood to growing up, discovering her body, and confronting the brutal reality of a woman's body being an object of sexual cravings.

napping underblanketing
young-nones

you know what it's called

(nie mam pojęcia tego w swoim
myślniku mowniku domowniku
u nas
nie istnieje
słownie ni dosłownie
tylko mój brat
coś
tam
ma)

cipka

(pierwsze słyszę peszy mnie odkrycie
szczeliny w moim bycie)

to
i ja
to
muszę
mieć

Warszawa, 19 października 2012

przesadzka

wybrzuszona
(brzemienna brzmienna przemienna)
sprowadzam
krew
pod nowy adres i składam w ofierze
(sprawdzam czy bierze)
bóle opatulam

(i have no idea not in my
thinkosaurus talkosaurus homesaurus
at home
it doesn't exist
literally or literarily
only my brother
has
something
there)

pussy

(never heard i'm miffed by the discovery
of the crack in my person)

i
must
also
have
it

Warsaw, 19 October 2012

exaggerant

The Polish title here has several facets: exaggeration, yes, but also movement, echoes of transplantation and perambulation. We chose to emphasise the idea of growth and excess, but the botanical motifs remain in the poem, in the hothouse, in the ripening and swelling. This is pregnancy connected to biology, to nature and its rhythms, and the religious vocabulary of sacrifice and divine inspiration only serves to stress how separate and distinct the two worlds are.

bulging
(pregnant resonant inconstant)
i bring
blood
to a new address and sacrifice
(check if it accepts)
wrap aches in a hothouse of

rąk
cieplarnią cierpliwą i parną
przytulam utulam
(niech śpi słodko/słono
łono i ono
no
niech no
tylko)

natknięta natchnięta wybrana
nabrzmiewam dojrzewam
odziewam
i urodziewam
(się)
na

no
we

Warszawa, ul. Asfaltowa, 3 września 2012

tabunowe tabuwanie

(brzydzą mnie
dziury otwory potwory
przedarte przetarte odrzuca
jak tylko
dotknę patrzeć
nie)
(ja tylko w spodniach
bo
tak
bezpieczniej

hands
patient and steamy
i smoothe i soothe
(lull it and the womb to dream
sweet/salty dreams sleep
well
let well
enough be)

known inspired chosen
i ripen i swell
i girth i put on
birth
(myself)

a
fre
sh

    Warszawa, ul. Asfaltowa, 3 September 2012

band banding

Almost all of this frantic, furtive poem happens in parentheses. With words which seem to conjure each other through alliteration and rhyme, Kamińska looks at the body as a liability, a risk, something to hide from yourself and others, something to fear — unless it's between women, where the two moments of respite are welcomed outside of the hushing brackets.

    (holes slits pits
      disgust me
  torn worn i scorn
     them when
   i touch don't
       look)
(always in trousers
       can't
        be
   overcareful

bez piecz nie i nie)
(mnie
śnił się
wąż mąż
przeraźliwie fałszywie
wił się
i gnał
strasznie się)
(mnie ze strzykawką i słoikiem
chciał mnie)
(za nic nie
zasnę pierwsza jeśli ktoś)
(boję się
rozchylić
uchylić
nachylić)

to
nic
nie
to tak tylko
kobiety kobietom
(z pokalania na pokalanie)

to
tylko
tak

pst

Warszawa, 20 września 2012

over and over care full)
(i
dreamt of a
serpent husband
frighteningly faithlessly
writhing
and wrenching
himself horribly)
(me with a syringe and a jar he
wanted me)
(no way i
fall asleep first if someone)
(i am afraid to
bare
broach
bend)

it's
no
thing
it's just
women to women
(from maculation to maculation)

it's
just
like

shh

Warsaw, 20 September 2012

czernowitz czarowidz

tu
szabas zaczyna się
od schuberta
(wieńczy
ślubem
lub bodaj
pojedynkiem)
woźnice z końmi
kłócą się o karla krausa
księgarń wyrosło więcej niż kawiarń i kwiaciarń
trotuary zamiata się wiązkami róż bądź burz
by kury mogły dziobać z nich
wiersze hölderlina

(ta mina!)

(inna
jest teraz
rzeczy
oczy
wistość
czyż)

(no
cóż)

(to
też
wiersz wiesz)

tagi: [ukraina] [bukowina] [czerniowce] [georg heintzen]

czernovitz charmovitz

This poem evokes the lost world of the Austro-Hungarian city now known as Chernivtsi in Ukrainian. Historically the city was called Cernăuți in Romanian, Czerniowce in Polish, Csernovic in Hungarian, Tshernovits in Yiddish and Chernovtsy in Russian, as it changed hands.

here
sabbath starts
with schubert
(ends with
a wedding
or at least
a duel)
coachmen
argue over karl kraus
more bookstores sprouted than coffeeshops and florists
pavements are swept with bundles of roses or thunder
so that chickens could peck
hölderlin's poems out of them

(that face!)

(reali
clari
ty
is different
now
is not)

(oh
well)

(that's
also
verse you see)

tags: [ukraine] [bukovina] [chernivtsi] [georg heintzen]

[:::]

odłamki macew
(masz
pomacaj
macę wymacaj
macicę z zarodkami liter
hebrajskich
rajskich
drzew i świec
złamanych załamanych zdławionych
dłoni
bo
nikt
ich
nie broni
bo to są
o n i)

tagi: [ukraina] [bukowina] [czerniowce] [sadogóra] [cmentarz żydowski]

[:::]

We are still in Chernivtsi, the poet now focusing her attention on the Jewish past of the city. She builds a network of alliteration mainly based around the letter 'm' and words relating to motherhood. She also employs a rhyme in the Polish between 'hebrajski' – 'rajski', that is 'Hebrew' and 'paradise'. This was probably the biggest translation challenge when working on this particular poem.

bits of matzeva
(here
touch
make out the matzo
the mother the embryos of letters
hebrew
brewed in paradise
trees and candles
broken heartbroken smothered
hands
for
no one
defends
them
for
it is
t h e m)

tags: [ukraine] [bukovina] [chernivtsi] [sadhora] [jewish cemetery]

koronauczycielka

z przyciętą nagle
przestrzenią
(szwy jeszcze widać
i ścieg pośpiesznie niedbały)

z odciętym dostępem do osób
(osobność i wsobność
tak łatwo
nastąpić zastąpić)

z naciskiem na miłość
– do technologii –
(wyszkol się sama w wielu językach
na jutro stań
specjalistką)

przykuta do krzesła
(krzyż krzyczy
i żebrze o masaż
poduszka ortopedyczna
potrzebna od teraz)

do skrzynki ze sprzętem
(posprzątać wcześniej też trzeba
co w kadrze w kamerze)
(ubrać się wystarczy
od góry)

zależna od przepływu
na łączach
(połączeń słyszeń i widzeń
jakości mnogości)

coronateacher

The poet, in this poem from Teraz zaraz, *enhances the atmosphere of fear and uncertainty by adding notes describing the number of new cases and deaths in Poland on particular days during the Covid pandemic. She talks about things we now associate with that time: masks, staying at home, conducting life and business through Zoom.*

the space
abruptly trimmed
(the seams still visible
and the stitch sudden and slapdash)

the access to people severed
(separateness and self-sufficiency
so easily
suppressed substituted)

stressing the love
– for technology –
(train yourself in many languages
turn into an expert
by tomorrow)

chained to a chair
(back is begging
moaning for a massage
orthopaedic pillow
needed from now on)

to a toolbox
(need to tidy up beforehand
what's in the frame in the camera)
(enough to only get dressed
on the top)

dependant on the transfer
along the wire
(connections of hearing and seeing
of quality plurality)

niepewna przepływu
przelewów
(w prognozach
raczej susze
niż sushi)

próbuję
matkować
czarnym kwadratom
na swoim
ekranie

Gocław, 28 czerwca 2020
[117. dzień epidemii w Polsce, 193 zakażonych, 3 zgony, w sumie
liczba zakażonych: 33907, zmarło: 1438]

wzdłuż / wszerz

wszelkim wszechświatem
teraz
muszę obejść się
pieszo

pobrzeże pokrzyw
świeżo stracona trawa
utrącone przez burzę
bukiety
czy też
kiście

sowicie lśnię więc liście
i zielenię
mierzwię wierzchołki drzew
i rzepaku

not sure of the transfer
of transfers
(forecasts forecast
drought rather
than dining out)

I try
to mother
the black squares
on my
screen

Gocław, 28 June 2020
[the 117th day of the pandemic in Poland, 193 new cases, 3 deaths,
altogether so far 33907 cases, 1438 deaths]

along / across

The poem meanders through language just like the speaker strolls through her city: making observations, bending rules, ignoring labels. Characteristically, the veneer of carefree word association conceals a meditation on the role of nature in a locked-down pandemic world; a slant ars poetica *built on 'choosing the long way'.*

i will now have
to go
without the universe
on foot

past nettle petals
freshly lost grass
bouquets
or maybe
bunches
laid low by the storm

so i give leaves a lavish shine
i green and
tousle treetops
buttercups

(trzepaka nie ma za to
chodziarz i narciarz
trenują
uparcie)

wiatr mi wyrywa
kartki
żeby
fruwały furkotały fyrtlowały
wierszyły się i mizdrzyły
brużdżąc powietrze

zbieram
(je
i się)

wybieram dłuższą drogę
nogę za nogą
przekładam
dokładam sterań i staram
się
iść
trwale

Gocław, kwiecień-czerwiec 2020

czyja ty jesteś

1.

wszystko było
inaczej
skurczone przestworza przestrzenie zwężone
zamknięta chałupa (firanki te

       (nobody batters rugs but
         walkers and skiers
              do train
            stubbornly)

          the wind steals my
                pages
               so they
            flit float flutter
         they poem and flatter
          furrowing the air

              i collect
             (them and
               myself)

         i choose the long way
           one foot in front
             of the other
          i shake every effort i
                try to
                  go
                 still

Gocław, April-June 2020

whose are you

A meditation in four chapters on the possibility of returning, this poem's dreamlike world is offset with hyperspecific detail: the quintessentially Polish riverside landscape, the string curtains, the tone of the other voice all combine to create a sense of realism among all the mist and the glow. We left some detail out: the original's 'obwarzanki' are almost (but not quite) bagels, and it felt wrong to mislabel these rolls often sold at church fairs.

    1.

everything was
different
shrunken sky narrowed spaces
old house shut (string curtains still the

same)
studnia stała dalej podwórko było większe (tu mieszka
ten facet który
umarł)

   2.

krajobraz ze starej baśni
(wały nad wisłą wierzby pastwisko
wszędzie
złe
psy)
odkryty stryjek który żył siedem dni
ciężarne świnie doroczne cmentarne obwarzanki
(tylko w bagno nie wejdź)
martwa woda i martwe powietrze
zagłębianie się w chaszcze
odgarnianie mgły i
gałęzi

   3.

wieczorne wędrówki
po grobach (świecą własnym
blaskiem)
układanie siebie po śladach (wszędzie jest
blisko)

   4.

(ostatni raz cię
widziałam jak miałaś trzy latka ale
od razu
poznałam)

Ostrów – Wielącza, 10 listopada 2008
Warszawa, 26 kwietnia 2020

same)
the well was further the courtyard bigger (here lives
the man who
died)

   2.

landscape from an old tale
(the vistula's banks the sand the willows the grassland
bad
dogs
everywhere)
newly uncovered uncle only lived seven days
pregnant pigs yearly cemetery bread
(don't you go walking in the swamp)
dead water and dead air
going deeper in the brushwood
brushing away mist and
branches

   3.

evening trips
to see the graves (aflame with their own
glow)
arranging yourself along the tracks (everywhere is
close)

   4.

(last time i
saw you you were three but
i knew you straight
away)

     Ostrów – Wielącza, 10 November 2008
     Warsaw, 26 April 2020

celuję cechuję

tłumaczka to czasem
gaśniczka
miłośniczka pokoju
(własnego wspólnego ogólnego)

a czasami rozpalaczka
palących pilących potrzebujących
historii
(chętniej herstorii)

podżegaczka pożarów
obszarów wrażliwych
(chętnie drażliwych)
wyraźliwych
zwykle
obraźliwie

czasem wrzaskunka
czasem szeptunka

piastunka
nieustanna
ostatnich
sztuk

stuk stuk
w liter
sznurki

zawsze
tam
gdzie
trze

ba

Warszawa, 20-21 lipca 2020

i aim i claim

Here, Kamińska speaking as a translator and as a woman, opens with the gendered word, 'tłumaczka', thus refusing the role's traditional invisibility, recognising that she can make her presence in the text known at the top of her lungs. We found an interesting challenge with the hollerer / healer dichotomy: the Polish 'wrzaskunka' is a neologism built out of 'wrzask', (scream) and 'szeptunka' (folk healer) has 'whisper' as the root. We prioritised the alliteration to reflect the original's pulsing, driving rhyme.

the translator she can be
an extinguisher
keeper of order
(logical natural pecking)

or an igniter of
burning pressing dire
histories
(preferably herstories)

starter of fires
in sensitive areas
(preferably overly sensitive)
expressitive
normally
insensitive

sometimes hollerer
sometimes healer

stalwart
holder
of the last
map

tap tap
on the
strings

of letters
always
so
ex

act

Warsaw, 20-21 July 2020

jestem mostem

ten dreszcz
deszcz
przeszywający
przepływający po ciele
gdy
trzeba
mieć dla siebie
ten wiersz
wersów
wersję swojską
teraz zaraz
bo się nie zaśnie
nie spocznie
nie nie
nie spożyje
nie żyje

tę chwilę
przyłapać przyszpilić
jej ważność uważność odgadnąć
łagodnym wzrokiem odgarnąć
jej włosy z czoła
palcami czułymi
z cyrylicy
wyłowić wyłonić
delikatne
płody
wody
łonowe
i nowe
nadać
jej
w
imię

Warszawa, 19 lipca 2020

i am a bridge

Translation is shown here as an organic act, a primal urge, an irresistible flow, a fascination, a creative spasm which results in something delicate being born. The breathless opening lines slow down as the focus shifts from the need to the text itself, and the loving contemplation ends with a joyful dismissal of grammar in the search for the right words.

that shiver
a river
flowing
going over the body
when
you
have to have
this poem
own your
own verse version
right away
or no sleep
no rest
no no
no bread
no breath

pin down
this instant its
importance divine its portents
with a soft gaze brush away
fringe from forehead
with gentle fingers
search cyrillics
finally find
fragile
fruit
of the
womb
waters
and give
her a
new in
the name

Warsaw, 19 July 2020

* * *

ostrzał rakietowy
przeżyła szafka kuchenna
w borodziance
i całkiem nieźle
trzyma się
ściany

i kogucik
nawet się nie zachwiał
majolikowy
z wasylkowa

i dzbanki
i talerze na suszarce
niewzruszenie
w pozycji
pionowej

pytacie
o namiary
producentów

made in ukraine
moi drodzy

twarde bo
ukraińskie

Warszawa, 9 kwietnia 2022

* * *

Poems from Pokój z widokiem na wojnę *are quite different from Aneta Kamińska's usual linguistic playfulness. The language is simpler and more direct, marked with a striking urgency – not surprising, since these are basically stories collected after the war broke out from the poet's numerous Ukrainian friends and acquaintances. The poet writes about kitchen appliances and tableware which survived a bombing. She mentions a rooster made of majolica, which we decided to change to plain pottery in English, since the term 'majolica' is less commonly used in English than in Polish.*

what survived the rocket fire
in borodyanka
was a kitchen cupboard
which still
clings
to the wall

and a rooster
it didn't even budge
a pottery one
from vasylkiv

and jugs
and plates on a drainer
unmoved
in an upright
position

you want
to know
the manufacturer

made in ukraine
my dears

ukrainian strong
through and through

Warsaw, 9 April 2022

* * *

co myśli żona
rosyjskiego żołnierza
który właśnie po raz kolejny gwałci
ukraińską kobietę

tylko niech wróci cało do domu?
tylko niech mi stamtąd przywiezie futro?
dlaczego tak rzadko dzwoni?

co myśli matka
rosyjskiego żołnierza
który właśnie wypala oczy
ukraińskim cywilom

żeby się tylko nie przeziębił?
czy dobrze go tam karmią?
niech bóg ma go w swojej opiece?

co myśli córka
rosyjskiego żołnierza
który właśnie strzela w głowę
ukraińskiemu dziecku

kiedy tato wróci z podróży?
czy przywiezie mi ładne zabawki?
czy zrobi tam ciekawe zdjęcia?

co myśli syn
rosyjskiego żołnierza
który właśnie kieruje rakietę
w ukraiński szpital położniczy

***

> *Here the poet creates a shocking reconstruction of thoughts of people related to a Russian soldier at war in Ukraine. We've all heard of terrible atrocities committed there; the poet attempts to recreate the thinking of the people on the perpetrator side. Despite the rawness of the topic, the poem is full of sarcasm.*

what goes through the head of a wife
of a russian soldier
who is right this second raping
a ukrainian woman yet again

just come home safe and sound?
bring me a fur coat?
why don't you call more often?

what goes through the head of a mother
of a russian soldier
who is right this second burning out
the eyes of ukrainian civilians

just don't catch a cold?
are you being fed well?
may god look after you?

what goes through the head of a daughter
of a russian soldier
who is right this second shooting
a ukrainian child in the head

when will dad be back from this trip?
will he bring me nice toys?
will he take some interesting pictures?

what goes through the head of a son
of a russian soldier
who is right this second aiming a rocket
at a ukrainian maternity hospital

czy przywiezie mi czołg albo karabin?
mój tato to bohater?
będę taki jak on?

Warszawa, 10 kwietnia 2022

sen mara

śnią mi się ciała
wybrakowane zamarłe powykręcane w zbiorowym
grobie w workach i na rowerach ledwo
okryte czerwoną
gliną

śnią mi się ciała
kobiet i dzieci rozebrane rzucone na kupę
opon jeszcze nie
spalone

śnią mi się detale
kobieca dłoń z manicurem hybrydowym różowy dziecięcy
klapek ręce związane szmatą kawałek
głowy

coś mi się przywidziało
myślę we śnie
chyba przesadzam

will he bring me a tank or a gun?
is my dad a hero?
will i be like him?

> Warsaw, 10 April 2022

all a dream

> *This poem tries to make sense of news about the Bucha massacre in the way we make sense of dreams: trying to remember details and stitching them together into a meaningful scene or story. The horrors are impossible to accept, and the poem turns to familiar details, houses, names, addresses, ending on the names of three internationally renowned Russian writers, taking on a new significance in the gruesome context of the preceding stanzas.*

i dream of bodies
incomplete unmoving twisted in a mass
grave in bags and on bikes barely
covered in red
clay

i dream of bodies
women and children undressed piled on some
tyres but not yet
burned

i dream of details
a woman's hand with hybrid manicure a child's pink
flip-flop hands tied with a rag a piece of
head

i am imagining things
i think in my dream
i must be exaggerating

kto by po nich czołgiem jeździł
kto by im uszy i nosy obcinał
kto by je gwałcił na śmierć albo po śmierci

to musi być bucza
poznaję nowe bloki
market fora i drogę do parku

więc to pewnie sąsiedzi
kocarewów panasiuków pryłuckich

a to ulice
puszkina
lermontowa
gorkiego

Warszawa, 4 kwietnia 2022

who would run over them with a tank
who would cut off their ears and noses
who would rape them to death or after death

this must be bucha
i know the new high-rises
the supermarket the way to the park

so these must be the neighbours
of the kotsarevs the panasiuks the prylutskis

and these are streets named after
pushkin
lermontov
gorky

> *Warsaw, 4 April 2022*

Biographical Notes

Aneta Kamińska is a Polish poet and a translator of Ukrainian poetry into Polish. She was born in Szczebrzeszyn, raised in Zamość and currently lives in Warsaw. She studied Polish Studies at the University of Warsaw and now teaches Polish as a second language.

She has published nine collections of her own poetry as well as translations of a number of Ukrainian poets.

Anna Blasiak is a poet, translator and managing editor of the European Literature Network. Anna writes poetry in Polish and in English. She has published two volumes of her own work, as well as translating over 40 books from English into Polish, including a number of children's and young adult books. She has also translated fiction and non-fiction from Polish into English (including Maciej Hen's *According to Her*, shortlisted for the EBRD Literature Prize 2023) as well as poetry between Polish and English.

Her work has been published in literary magazines and she regularly reviews books in translation for the European Literature Network.

Bohdan Piasecki is a poet and translator from Poland with a particular interest in multilingual writing and voice as a medium for poetry. He founded the first poetry slam in Poland in 2003, before moving to the UK to pursue a doctorate in translation studies. A prolific performer, he has toured in over 27 countries and in 2023 he won the inaugural Forward Prize for Best Single Poem - Performed. He has translated numerous contemporary performance poets for the stage, and recently worked with the Manchester Poetry Library to curate their Polish collection.

Bohdan teaches Creative Writing at the University of Birmingham.